THE PRESENCE

OF THE LIGHT

Before me stretches the Path of Light
I see the way.
Behind me lies the mountain path
With stones and cobbles on the way.
Around me are the thorns.
My feet are tired.
But straight ahead streams the lighted way
And I am on that Way.

(Ancient prayer from the Tibetan)

THE

PRESENCE

OF

THE LIGHT

by Annabel Chaplin
aka Anabelle Markson

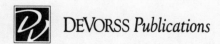
DEVORSS *Publications*

© 1994 by Annabelle Markson

ISBN: 0-87516-676-8
Library of Congress Card Catalog No.: 94-68112

DeVorss & Company, Publisher
P.O. Box 550 — Marina del Rey, CA 90294

Printed in the United States of America

Contents

To the Inner Teacher

Also by Annabel Chaplin:

The Bright Light of Death

Preface

The stories in this book are all true. The personalities, most of whom are still alive, have consistently been told to credit the healings and the improvement in their lives to the Light, which makes all things possible.

I cannot take credit for something that comes naturally to me. I know, on the deepest level of knowing, that the Light of love and wisdom is the source of all that is good, true and beautiful — the source of LIFE itself. All I did was to learn how to respond to its directions, its influence, its power. And the more I accepted, trusted and responded, the more evident the manifestations of the Light became.

And at ninety, I am still learning, still searching.

Introduction

Ever since my first book, *The Bright Light of Death*, was published, I have been bombarded with requests for another book. "Please write about your other experiences — about your work with all of us, the living."

For a long time I felt no urge to write again. I knew from my past writing experience that I needed to be inspired, uprooted from my comfortable niche, if I was to surrender my comforts and my sleep to the demands of the task. I remembered well the sleepless nights — the inspiring moments always seemed to come at night when all was quiet, when my own restless mind was still. I remembered the frenzy of trying to write in longhand the words that came flooding into my mind, thoughts of how to organize the wealth of material stored in my subconscious. The only way I could write a new book would be to follow the same pattern. But I had no desire to write; I had no definite plan of procedure. I felt that when the time came for me to surrender to the urgings of my friends, I would know it. Now that time has come.

It came about in the last place in the world I would have thought it could happen.

I was visiting in Boston with some of my very old and dear friends. Two people are responsible. One, a charming, beautiful lady, approached me as the party was breaking up.

"I've just heard that you have written a book about the Light," she said. "I hear so much about the Light — please tell me more." There was only time for an exchange of addresses and a promise from me to mail her a copy of my book.

The second person was an old friend who scoffed at anything religious or spiritual. He thought that people who believe in an Invisible Universe, a God, a life beyond death, were deluding themselves. He directed his barbs at me. He went on and on downgrading all my beliefs.

I was heartsick for him and for anyone who could be so cynical, so rigid in their concepts that they do not even ask pertinent questions of me, or take into account the many intelligent men and women who have researched these subjects. This man had not even read any of the countless books on the subject of his scorn — books written by illustrious men and women through the centuries. He had not even heard of the psychical research conducted by William James, that famous psychology professor of his Alma Mater. He had come to definite conclusions on a subject about which he had no knowledge beyond hearsay.

In my personal life I have always been surrounded by disbelievers, but all of them have had some degree of openness, some degree of curiosity, some areas of belief. This particular man was the first one, in a very long time, who was so convinced that he did not even challenge me. It was a new experience for me.

It has taken years of dedication, research, studying, and discussion for me to have come to some of my conclusions. Even those of us deeply involved in our beliefs do not agree on every detail, but we are always open to debate. I, too, was New-England born and bred, and had my share of typical New-England conservatism — a conservatism that helped me to separate the bizarre from the valid; that often made me skeptical of ideas until I could find satisfactory evidence. But once convinced, shown by the results in my own life and in the lives of others, I accepted. The Doubting Thomas in me always asked for proof, and the Inner Teacher — the Great Light — never failed to point the way, which I was free to accept or reject.

So I pleaded with my dear good friend — keep an open mind. So little to ask; so much to gain. "Keep the door open a crack, for even a crack will let some light in."

It is because of those who want to know more about the Light, and skeptics whose minds are "a little open," that I decided to write this book. But there is a larger reason too. I am writing about my experiences because I believe there are some things in this prosaic world of ours that have to be told in order to offset the prevalent mood of despair and gloom, the universal feeling of discouragement and hopelessness over humanity's apparent trend toward destruction.

Living in a world inhabited by so many violent, angry, fearful individuals, constantly bombarded by threats of a nuclear war, we begin to believe in Armageddon, total annihilation. Although my rational mind tells me that such a dire end of mankind is possible, something within me remains serenely optimistic. So for those who will read these words, I humbly state that as long as there is Goodness in the world, there is hope; and I firmly believe that Universal Goodness exists and always will.

Chapter I

The Great Bright Light

Much has been written and said about the Light. Throughout the centuries, there have been individuals who have had the subjective experience of the Light — generally referred to as *the mystical experience*. These experiences are always different, but there is one similarity — it is extremely difficult to express the event in the language of our culture.

I will attempt to describe my own mystical experience of the Light, knowing full well it cannot be easily conveyed in words. For these many long years (38), I have not spoken of it. First of all, because of reluctance to reveal a sacred experience; and secondly, because I know that ordinary language has no words to describe it. I can state with certainty, however, that the experience of the Light lifted me out of my rigid concepts and everyday life into a dimension of a Reality that changed the whole course of my life and enabled me to accept mystical concepts without rebellion.

* * *

I had been meditating for a few months, and had just been released from binding ties by my Dream of Liberation, when the earthshaking experience of the Great Light occurred.

It was dawn. I was abruptly awakened by an enormous, formless, Great Bright Light moving toward me. It was solid. It was real. Coming from a blue sky high above, it moved closer and closer. Powerless, I had no time to question or be fearful, no strength nor desire to pull away. It was about to enter my right side. Its approach was quick and authoritative. I began to experience a sublime feeling of total love as the Light penetrated and took full possession of me.

Words are completely inadequate to describe the exquisite feeling of that moment. It has to be experienced to be understood. The true mystical experience can't be talked about or analyzed or formulated in words. So for me to describe the totality of my emotions in that glorious moment when the Great Light of the Universe absorbed me would be impossible. It is reminiscent of that joyous feeling of giving and receiving when in the embrace of one's true mate, reminiscent of that supreme act of love when one is so totally immersed that there is no he or she, no you or I — but only *one*.

The act of pure true love between a man and a woman is probably the most gratifying, beautiful, overwhelming experience in the physical universe, but the union with the Great Light is infinitely more exalting, infinitely more beautiful, infinitely more ecstatic — it is a feeling of oneness on a superhuman, divine level.

In that supernatural union the *I* of me no longer

existed. Totally immersed in the light of love, the *I* disappeared—and only when the Light departed from the opposite side of me did I become aware of my existence in the material world. I knew and could describe the moments before the entrance, the ecstatic moment of the entrace, and the departure. But during the absorption in the Light, the *I*—mind and body—dissolved. There was no *I* to feel, think or describe.

The Light left. I was alone again—the Great Light of love had moved on. A part of me was kneeling by the bedside in prayer. Another part of me was in a daze. Another part of me felt powerful, as though I could conquer the world, right all the wrongs, help elect good people to rule the world. Basking in the memory of the Great Light, I felt that nothing was impossible. Everyone could be happy, there could be no hunger and poverty, the world could be at peace, if only everyone would allow that magnificent Light to come into their life.

I remained still for hours in a glow of joy and bliss. I felt humble and exalted at the same time. I became a new human being.

The experience was earthshaking—literally—and for a few months I lived on a high plateau of joy. My feet barely touched the ground. How could it be otherwise? There I was, a creature of habit and impulses, rooted deeply in materiality—a little boat on the great sea of life, tossed about by the whims of nature. And now, suddenly, I was free of all worldly desires, free of negative ties, free of insurmountable problems—no longer yearning for what I could not have, no longer searching for answers to a riddle beyond my ability to solve, no longer striving for the impossible. I was joyously, incredibly happy. I felt loved—loved in spite of my faults, weaknesses and inadequacies.

For months I lingered in memory in a blue sky of joy. I could have stayed there forever, but that wisdom which was beyond me deemed otherwise. I slowly came back to my little boat on the vast sea of life. But now I, the passenger, became I, the captain. For the first time in my life I chose the course. I handled the anchor. I learned how to steer the little boat (the little me) and direct it in all kinds of weather. For the first time in my adult life I felt whole, capable, strong; and I knew that never again would I be drifting aimlessly, victimized by my own sense of inadequacy and inferiority, my "nothingness." I was no longer a nothing, for I had been accepted and loved by the Great Being of Light. Nothing else mattered.

And so I returned to the storms of life. My learning began. First of all, I learned that the Light which had absorbed me was to become the guiding Light of my life; that when I turned to It for help, It was always there. It always was and always will be. I had to learn how to trust It. I had to learn how to turn to It in time of turmoil and in time of quiet. Later I came to call It my Inner Teacher.

I made many mistakes. I still do. The child undertaking a new study makes errors, but by diligent application and devotion to his study finally learns his lessons. As time went on, I became accustomed to "looking within." I called it "letting life show the way." I became aware of the importance of each event, each confrontation. No event, small or great, ever again seemed insignificant.

Everything was important. And because the Great Being of Light cared, each and every human being was important. All I, we, had to do was to accept Its presence and enter into that stream of Light pouring out Its beneficent energy of love.

From that moment on, I have endeavored to achieve a balance between the spiritual and material worlds. I was taught in my meditations that one was as important as the other. I live in the material world and it is in that world that I must function and apply the spiritual values. Finally I had embarked on the great adventure of living in the here and now.

I began to meditate daily — in the morning, noon, and at dusk. I was settling in with a wonderful feeling of contentment. Due to events beyond my control, my outer life was in turmoil, but my inner life remained serene. I brought that serenity to the problems of my everyday life, and seemingly insurmountable difficulties became endurable. My husband and other people around me benefited and began to turn to me for help. I always knew that when they came to me for help they were receiving answers from the Inner Teacher, not from the "little me" (the personality self).

* * *

As time went on, the meditations began to change. I was not allowed to bask serenely in the downy softness of my contentment. I was shown in imagery and in dreams that I must begin to share my new-found knowledge with others. At first I laughed. I was a novice. There were so many qualified teachers around far more advanced and capable than I. No one needed me. Although I rebelled at the thought of public exposure, yet I felt an over-whelming desire that everyone should find the inner peace and joy that I had found.

My meditations began to be more specific: How to help others would be revealed to me. Trust the Light. It will show the way. I did not have to barge into the world in any big dramatic fashion (that was a relief). Events in my everyday life would occur which would indicate the direction I should take. The reflection of the inner power that was given to me from that glorious experience of the Great Light would attract diverse people. All I had to remember was to "look within" for answers. Each person's problems could be presented to the Light for solutions or understanding. I had to learn to accept my role of interpreter and mediator. The Inner Teacher would always be with me teaching, guiding, sustaining, and I would be given the evidence needed for me to understand and accept my role. Little did I know then how dramatic and extraordinary the evidence would be.

I may doubt myself and I often do, but I learned and acknowledged that anything and everything that comes from the Light, the Inner Teacher, is true, is important, is honest. And never for one moment did I doubt the power of the Great Light, the wisdom of the Inner Teacher.

Chapter II

The Healing Power of the Light

It seems as though Universal Goodness knows us better than we do, knows what is acceptable to us and what might easily be ignored or rejected. I did not have to go out into the world for my first experience with the power of the Light. It came about in my own home.

At that time my husband was having serious financial difficulties. He was struggling to hold on to a business which he had spent 25 years of his life building—25 years of long hours, hard work and sacrifices. Now at 50 years of age, his life's ambitions were being shattered. He was devastated, his strong ego diminished. It was painful for me to stand by and observe his suffering, but I was fortified by the inner Light. Difficult as this particular lesson was, I believed that everything happens for a purpose. I tried to convey to him that he could weather the storm if only he held on to a belief in himself and his ability to handle any difficult situation. I emphasized to him that he still had the same keen sharp mind that had always served him well. It was important for him to avoid self-recriminations and despair.

Each day I meditated for him. The temptation to ask

11

the Light for his immediate success, for specific results, tormented me. I desired above all else to work some magic for him. I wanted to plead and beg the Universe for his success, to ease his suffering. But that kind of meditation or prayer was against my understanding of the Spiritual Law of the Universe. Just as the Great Light, the God force, does not coerce us into doing anything contrary to our free will, so must we realize that we cannot coerce or bend the Light, or God, if you will, to our desires. Although at that time a beginner in meditation, I knew that the most I should ask for was strength and faith. So I meditated for that which would be "right and best" for him to come about. I believed that this event in his life was far less important than the great lesson he was about to learn from his difficult experience.

How many times, then and now, have I been tempted to fall into the trap of my wishful desires! But I always tried to resist, and I taught my students never to ask for what they think *they* want, but instead ask for what is "right and best," and for the the strength to accept it. The Universal Goodness knows better what experience we must have in order to evolve and grow in consciousness.

So I meditated in this way for my husband. As always, my meditation gave me the strength I needed for the crisis in our lives. And then came a week of devastating blows. "Everything is turning sour," he complained. And finally his physical body protested; the strain took its toll.

One night he came home bent over in great pain. I hurriedly helped him into bed and called the doctor. When I described the symptoms, the doctor offered to come to the house. House calls were rare, so I knew that the doctor must have sensed that it was necessary to see his patient immediately. By this time my husband was writhing in terrible pain. Upon examination the doctor diagnosed the condition as a very severe ulcer. "A second-year medical student could diagnose this one," he said.

"I knew it," my husband replied. "It feels like the one I had 20 years ago, but this one is much worse."

After prescribing a pill to alleviate the pain the doctor took his leave. As I was seeing him to the door he again repeated to me: "A second-year medical student could easily diagnose this case. I want you to bring him to the office in the morning for some X-rays."

I gave the pain-relieving pill to my husband and then went into the room in which I habitually meditated. I recall that meditation quite clearly. For no reason that I knew of then, I sought to establish that wonderful feeling of oneness. I quieted my agitated mind and body and asked for the Light to give me the strength and the guidance to know what to do and how best to help him. I visualized the Light of healing surrounding him.

I returned to my poor husband. He was again moaning and groaning in great pain. It was awful. I gave him another pain-killer pill and sat quietly beside him as I waited for the codeine to work. I gently touched his swollen abdomen, kissed him and said, as one would to a child, "try to sleep—you will feel better in the morning." I checked in on him several times during the night and as the moaning and groaning ceased, I too retired.

Early in the morning I was awakened by someone laughing. Laughing?—or was it crying? I dashed out of bed into the dressing room where the sound emanated, and found my husband standing in front of the mirror pounding his stomach with his fists and saying, "A second-year medical student!" When he saw me staring in amazement as he attacked his erstwhile tender stomach, he pointed a finger at me and said, "Was it you? Careful, you better not think it was something you did!"

Now I was startled. "Something *I* did" — I didn't do anything — all I did was meditate for him and touch him. Was *this* a demonstration of the healing power of the Light? I had read about spiritual healings, "laying on of hands," and miracle cures wrought by prayer. "More things are wrought by prayer than the world dreams of." My husband interrupted my inner thoughts.

"Should I go to the doctor's office for the X-rays?" he asked me.

I did not know what to say and frankly told him so.

He decided to keep the appointment and I went to consult the psychologist with whom I was studying at that time. When I finished telling the psychologist the entire story of the strange event, he quietly said, "The doctor will find no ulcer. Your husband has had a so-called spiritual healing. You are a healer." He proceeded to give me some books on healing and indicated that there were certain procedures I would have to learn in order to develop this gift.

"A healer" — as grateful as I was for the prognosis that my husband was cured, and as awed as I was by the healing power of the Light, at the same time I was nonplussed by the personal significance of being placed in the role of a healer. As much as I wanted my husband to be cured (the cure was permanent — he never had another attack) and relieved of his agonizing pain, so much was I reluctant to become a healer. From what I had seen of the healers around Los Angeles and on TV, I didn't see how I could espouse that profession.

The healing had a significant effect upon my husband. He attacked his failing business affairs with renewed vigor and optimism. That night we celebrated by going to dine at our favorite restaurant. Eating the Indonesian lamb, I looked up to find my husband staring at me as though seeing me for the first time. It was a look of disbelief and wonderment. He leaned over and kissed me, saying simply, "Thank you."

MILLIE

In all these long years that I have been involved in spiritual work I have noticed that new lessons and new experiences always come in rapid succession, all bearing a significant message on the same theme, as though to imprint the truth of it emphatically upon my mind.

All through the years of my concentrated effort in the work, Millie has been an important contributor to my growth. She was the first one after my experience with the Light to seek my help and the first member of the Tuesday meditation group. From the beginning, she absorbed the spiritual teaching and applied it with a depth of understanding and acceptance beyond the usual. She is one of the dearest, most loving persons I have ever known.

I was in my study working with a colleague when I received a desperate call from Millie.

"Please, Annabel, can I see you immediately. I am in the doctor's office and I have just received terrible news." She was sobbing. "Can I come over?"

"Of course, come right away. I'll be waiting for you at the door."

In ten minutes Millie was in my arms weeping uncontrollably. I held her and comforted her as best I could. By this time I too was upset and anxious. I begged her to tell me what had happened at the doctor's office.

"I have just been given a death blow," she sobbed out. "Dr. S. (coincidentally my husband's doctor) says that the X-rays show that my kidneys have reached the point of no return and that momentarily I could have a complete breakdown of their functions."

Now we both wept. Not Millie, I thought—good, kind, loving Millie—dear God, please not Millie. I was devastated.

Suddenly a thought flashed into my overwrought emotions.

"Wait a minute, Millie," I said excitedly, hopefully, "remember my husband's ulcer healing last week?" Of course she knew all about it; she was one of the few people in whom I confided.

"Don't give up. We won't give up. We are going to try the same treatment for you."

My colleague's help was enlisted, for she was a firm believer in spiritual healing. The three of us meditated. Millie was calmer now. We all entered into the silence and established, each in our own way, our relationship with the Universal Light. After the meditation my friend and I put our hands on Millie's body in the area where the kidneys are located. We quietly talked about the spiritual power and some of our experiences, all the while keeping our hands on Millie's body. Knowing full well that *we* do not do the healing, we simply relaxed and let *It* do the work.

My hands became burning hot. Shooting pains went up and down my arm, my shoulders ached. The pain mounted. I let it happen. Something inside me knew that it was all right. I held my hands on Millie's body until the awful pain in my body subsided. When it did, I surmised that the healing treatment was over. The moment I removed my hands from the kidney area, the pain in my body vanished. I had read somewhere that after a treatment, a healer should wash the hands. So I did. It was my first healing experience of that kind.

Millie came the allotted number of times that we had scheduled. With each treatment the heat in my hands and the pain in my body lessened, and when I no longer felt the discomfort, I knew that my work was finished.

I told Millie, "We have done what we were shown to do and now it is in the hands of the Universal Goodness, the Light." She was optimistic and hopeful, not only because she believed in spiritual healing, but also because she was feeling better.

The doctor had told her to return in a month for more X-rays. On the day scheduled for her check-up Millie called and asked me whether she should keep her appointment. She explained that she did not want to take the X-rays yet, as *she* felt that more time was needed for "God's work to be done." I told her that it was a decision she had to make and to follow her own intuition. She decided to cancel the appointment and told the secretary she would make another one shortly.

Fortunately Docter S. is a very busy man and did not realize that his patient with the imminent kidney failure had neglected to report back for further X-rays. Eight months later Millie was in the hospital for minor surgery. Checking her records, Doctor S. caught the omission and hurriedly ordered kidney X-rays before surgery. To his utter and complete amazement there was no sign of his patient's former kidney damage. He ordered another X-ray—the same good news. Millie's kidneys were completely cured—normal.

I arrived at the hospital shortly after the good news had been given to her. We were overjoyed, jubilant. Some nurses and staff doctors came into the room, looked at Millie and left, all of them bewildered and in a state of disbelief. The news spread around the hospital. More doctors came to read the before and after X-rays. They had never seen a reversal of this kind.

I felt sorry for Doctor S. This was his second exposure to a miracle healing in which somehow he suspected I was involved, for he asked Millie to tell me he would like me to come to his office. He wanted to talk to me. I sent him a note stating I would love to see him at any time, but his busy office was not the right place for the kind of information I was willing to give him. I hinted that I knew he was puzzled by the two healings and I hoped I could enlighten him.

He never replied.

The important fact was that Millie's cure was complete and now, many years later, there is not a trace of any kidney damage.

Even though the before and after X-rays proved something extraordinary had happened, medical science seems unable to deal with an occurrence that does not fit into its training and knowledge.

I can hardly blame the doctors. I too find it difficult to understand.

FRANCES

Frances was an acquaintance whom I had met many times at the homes of mutual friends. Somehow I never could warm up to her. Being a gregarious person, I really like most people, but there is a certain type of woman who intimidates me. I secretly call them the male-female-type. The are perfectly normal women, but they have many characteristics of the male. They are usually bright, efficient, aggressive, self-confident and capable. I instinctively shy away from them.

Frances was this type of person, so when a mutual friend told me that Frances was very ill with cancer and wanted to see me, I was taken aback. Our mutual friend, Sally, had just come from a short visit with Frances and went into detail about the extent of her illness. I knew that she had had a breast removed, but Sally explained the latest developments. Six months after the breast removal, further X-rays showed that the cancer had metastasized and spread throughout her body, far beyond the confines of the breast. Dr. C., a well-known Los Angeles doctor, had advised more intensive and somewhat dangerous surgery which required the expertise of another nationally famous doctor. As that doctor was out of the country, the operation was delayed for six weeks until his return.

Frances, in great pain, was confined to her bed.

When Sally visited her, Frances asked about me, saying that she had seen me some months ago at a lecture on extrasensory perception. She told Sally that she hadn't known that I was interested in that subject. Sally proceeded to inform Frances that it was a deeper involvement than a mere passing interest. She briefly told her about my meditation classes and how participation in a group had helped her. Frances was curious and eager to know more and said that she would like to see me. Sally conveyed the message to me.

I promised Sally I would make the call, which I promptly did, and we made an appointment for the next day.

I was shocked at the change in poor Frances. She was pale and haggard, her pain visible on her face. Her upper right side was heavily bandaged and she explained that her shoulder and arm hurt so much when she moved that it was more comfortable having the arm strapped to her body. She asked many questions about my beliefs, my work, my groups, and then told me her interests, the books she was reading. Soon we were deeply involved in my favorite subject. I left promising to return soon again. No mention of healing was made. I avoided that subject. I was still somewhat intimidated by her.

As I walked away from Frances' home, the little voice of conscience reproached me — "Coward, Coward." I admitted the accusation and perhaps anybody else but Frances would have been "treated."

That night I was awakened with the most excruciating pain imaginable; the entire right side of my upper body was gripped in an intolerable pain. As I squirmed and groaned, the little voice again said, "Coward," and then I knew that I was experiencing Frances' pain. I also knew what I had to do on my next visit.

On the following day, as soon as I entered Frances' room, I began to talk about spiritual healing. I sheepishly confessed that I seemed to have become a channel for healing. I hastened to tell her that in the short time that I had been involved, a few people were helped and some were not — I confessed that I never knew why some and not others. It did not even seem to matter whether or not they were believers in the mystical. That too puzzled me. For that reason I was in a quandary as to how to proceed. But I never refused anyone who asked. She immediately broke in and said, "I am asking. Please try. What have I to lose?"

I meditated for a moment, called upon the Great Light for help, and put my hand on her breast and shoulder. In a few minutes that awful pain came into me. Frances with her eyes closed and somewhat relaxed did not see me squirming. The pain kept mounting. My hands seemed to be in a tight vise, glued to her body — I had never experienced such terrible pain. Just when I thought that I could hardly endure more, it began to subside and then I knew the "treatment" was over. I left the room for the customary ritual of washing the hands.

I returned to find Frances a little more relaxed. She thanked me and I agreed to return in a few days for the next "treatment." I told her that I thought it would take several more treatments before we could feel we had done our part. Before I left I reminded her that the results are not in our hands. Again she said, "We have nothing to lose. Thank you for trying."

As I expected, with each treatment the pain that was seemingly transferred to me lessened, and on the third treatment subsided considerably. I left, reminding Frances not to talk about the treatments to anyone, and she promised to call me whenever she felt like it.

A week later Frances called to report that she was feeling "a little better" and had more mobility in her right arm. Each week she reported she had more mobility and was feeling better. On the fourth week she reported being able to use her right hand and arm without pain, and in general the pain was letting up. She was able to sleep at night without sleeping pills.

An appointment had been set up with Dr. C. for further X-rays prior to arranging for the major operation. When Frances walked into the doctor's office, impishly swinging her right arm in wide circles, she reveled in the drama of seeing the stunned expression on the doctor's face. He immediately ordered X-rays and again he was astounded. He had never experienced a reversal of this nature. He informed her there was no need for the operation. She was cured. He hugged her and exclaimed, "This is a miracle — a miracle."

A year later Frances' other breast was removed. She was acutely disappointed that the healing did not include the left breast, which was a simple condition compared to the one that had responded to the healing. I had no explanation either; but the so-called miracle added many more good years to her life.

* * *

In Millie's case the spiritual healing augmented her devotion to the God force; in Frances' case the disappointment of the second breast removal diminished her enthusiasm. In my husband's case, it opened his mind up to the possibility that there was something in the beyond which, although incomprehensible to his rational mind, still had affected him and made him aware that there could be "something to it." He later responded to several less dramatic healings. His new awareness was good for our marriage because he knew at first hand that what I was doing was constructive and good, even though he didn't really understand it. He respected my "work" and cooperatively encouraged my dedication to it.

Two things held me back from a healing career. First, and the more important, I could not understand why it worked for some and not for others. Why did Frances have a miraculous healing, and yet one year later the other breast had to be removed? Secondly, I felt that unless I could intuitively know who could be a successful candidate for healing, I couldn't take the risk of impos-

ing a cruel disappointment upon persons already bur-
dened with great pain. It might serve to increase their
despair and hopelessness, and might even make them feel
unworthy of God's attention.

Actually, I believed that this problem of healing working for some and not for others has to do with the individual's karma or destiny. But this is something not
easily explained, nor is it easy for a person who is suffering to accept. So I tried to prepare each candidate before the healing treatment by simply telling him or her
that sometimes it did not work for reasons which were as
mysterious to me as the fact that oftentimes it worked
miraculously.

I struggled with my reluctance to be the instrument of
such an uncertain method, and at the same time I rea-
soned that if the Light wanted me to be a channel for
healing, It would reveal the knowledge I needed in order
to go on with it. I also felt strongly that by temperament
and background I could not become a public healer like
the healers on TV and on the stage. I knew that the
Universe did not expect this of me, as my life moved in
a totally different pattern. I relaxed and gave everything
over to the Guiding Light. I watched the signs — Life
would show me the next step; it would reveal what was
right for me, consistent with my temperament, weaknesses and strengths. As time went on, I was shown other
areas in which I could serve, but the healing gift was
never neglected, and I continued to apply the healing
hands whenever I was asked.

Chapter III

The Light Shows the Way

Part 1 — A Lesson in Absent Healing

The experiences with healings never stopped and I was learning when, and with whom, I should allow myself to be a channel for the healing power.

As always, the Light, the inner teacher, showed me the way to serve by placing me in situations that were essential for my growth and understanding. I had to develop that discriminating faculty necessary for the kind of work I was doing then and in the future. Although my studies taught me the principles and the general rules, it was in the incidents and confrontations in everyday-life situations with all kinds of people that the inner teachings were put into action.

As I worked with people, I learned from each one how best I could apply my abilities and knowledge. People, their lives, their problems, became my life, my problems, and my teachers. From them and with them I learned the most.

Shortly after my first revelation, I was invited to join a group of women who were also meditating and searching for answers to life's puzzling situations. They were an intelligent group who believed in a superior power, call it what you will. It was reassuring for me to be in that congenial group. We shared our thoughts and experiences. The members had begun to accept my healing abilities, based on the miraculous events related in chapter 2, and were most supportive.

HOLLY

One day, as we were discussing the phenomenon of spiritual healing, Elsa, a member of the group, suggested that we meditate for a healing for her sister-in-law, Holly. Most of us had met Holly and knew of her affliction, her pretty face distorted by a facial paralysis of long standing. Elsa became quite enthusiastic. "Why don't we try to heal Holly? If it works for Holly, who has had this facial paralysis for years without any hope of getting better, wouldn't it be further proof that anything or anyone can be healed? Let's try it."

I hesitated. Elsa continued, "Mark (Holly's husband) will be sure to tell me if there is even a slight improvement. We must try it—think what it would mean to him if Holly is healed!"

It was a challenge. We agreed to try. Then and there we all decided to include a special healing meditation for Holly in our weekly meetings. It was also suggested that we meditate for her every day at a special time. In our concerted efforts, the unsuspecting Holly would be bombarded by healing vibrations.

At that time, it never occurred to any of us that we were interfering. That lesson came later.

Holly was the wife of a well-known man in our city. I knew him personally and admired him, not only for his worldly achievements, but also for his character. He was attractive, brilliant, and emotionally stable. He believed in God and man. He loved his fellow man, and in turn he was loved by all who knew him.

Partly because of her condition and partly because she was a talented writer, Holly became a semi-recluse. She devoted herself to writing, and buried herself all day long in her studio. Being extremely wealthy, she had no household chores, and emerged from her studio in the evenings in time for the family meal. She must have been very beautiful when she met and subsequently married Mark, but now her face was distorted by a paralysis which made her look somewhat grotesque. She had been afflicted with this malady since the birth of her first child some 18 years ago.

Undaunted by these discouraging facts, our group undertook the task of devoting our time and efforts to the unsuspecting recipient of our earnest ministrations.

Six weeks later, I received an excited and almost incoherent call from Elsa. Since she was habitually calm and well-spoken, I had difficulty relating the hysterical voice and unintelligible words with Elsa's characteristic tone. She calmed down.

"A miracle!—Holly is cured," she cried out excitedly. "Mark has just told me that the doctor reports that activity has been restored to Holly's facial muscles, and the nerve endings responded to his probings for the first time in many years. The doctor wants her to encourage this renewed activity by doing facial exercises. He is amazed and quite sure that with the prescribed exercise and manipulations she can be helped."

Naturally, our group was elated. We met to discuss our unique accomplishment. We remembered to offer prayers of gratitude to the healing power of God, and decided that from now on, we would include other difficult and incurable cases in our weekly meditations and meetings. We had a new mission. An exciting purpose!

But we did not reckon with Holly's unbelievable re-action to her doctor's suggestions. She adamantly refused to cooperate. When the news of Holly's rejection reached me, I couldn't understand it. Why? Why would anyone be so stubborn and indifferent to such an extraordinary and beneficial cure? Why wouldn't she want to be beau-tiful again — for her husband's sake? Didn't she under-stand that she had been given a gift from God? Did she dare ignore that gift? Of course, she didn't know about the spiritual healing. Therefore, she could not be faulted for her ingratitude. We had to tell her about the heal-ing meditation for her.

As Holly would not listen to Elsa, Elsa insisted that it was my duty to tell Holly about our meditations and ex-plain spiritual healing. I was reluctant to do it, and I wondered when or how to tell her. As was my custom, I relied on Life to show the way.

And it did.

A few weeks later my husband and I were invited to Holly and Mark's home for dinner. As we were the only ones invited, it was to be an intimate evening. Events in life do have a way of showing how and when to take action. Nervously I realized that this occasion was going to be a "moment of truth." In order to prepare my husband for what was coming, I told him the whole story. I confessed that I was going to inform Mark and Holly about the healing experiment. My husband listened and then discouragingly said, "I hope you know what you are doing."

I hated the idea of confronting Holly and Mark with what would seem to them a weird story, but I thought I must. I did not want to fail the Inner Teacher again by my lack of courage. ("The coward" had learned her lesson.)

After a delightful dinner and equally delightful conversation, I proceeded to tell Mark and Holly about our group's meditation for Holly. As strange as it must have seemed to him, Mark listened intently. He and I were very good friends. He knew that I was reliable and that the experience I described must have been gunuine. He interrupted me once or twice to ask pertinent questions, and when I was finished, he was first to speak up. I later recorded the conversation and its results so that I could inform the group.

"I have read and heard about such seeming miracles," he said. "The Bible and literature are full of these kinds of happenings. I have never experienced it first-hand, but I am open-minded, and I believe you."

My husband was so amazed and encouraged by Mark's reaction that he forgot his earlier misgivings, and proceeded to tell him all about the miraculous cure of his ulcer.

All this time Holly remained silent. Finally she spoke

up. "I don't want to be any part of this!" she exclaimed defiantly. "I like myself the way I am. I like my life the way it is! I am in a position to show the world that one of the most desirable men in this city adores me the way I am. I like seeing all the beauties trying to entice him and getting nowhere because he loves me despite all my defects. Our love for each other is so all-encompassing that I don't need to be beautiful in order for him to be faithful to me. Our love goes beyond the surface."

She was adamant. She was so positive and certain that I did not even try to convince her. She had already made her choice. She subsequently refused to cooperate with the doctor, and ignored his instructions.

The group was disappointed, to say the least, but it was a great and important lesson for me and, I hope, for them. After that never again did I participate in an un-asked-for healing. And no one in that group ever again suggested that we meditate for healing anyone who didn't ask. Instead, we meditated and prayed for the Light to show the way for those in need. If we knew of anyone who was suffering, we put that person in an orbit of light. We prayed for the Light to show each one his or her way, whatever that might be. Beyond that, we would not interfere!

*   *   *

I learned from the Holly experience that some people like their illnesses. It gives them a reason to be different, to indulge their own way of life. Holly enjoyed her work, her way of life, and even her affliction. There are countless other reasons why people resist help. Sometimes their illness serves their need for attention, a way of getting sympathy, and even a form of self-indulgence. Some feel unworthy of anything better than a life of suffering. And still others are convinced that it is their karma, their destiny. So be it.

I looked to the Light for guidance, to show me when to advance and when to retreat. I believed that the Light could and would guide me as long as I kept the channel open. I concluded every morning meditation with my favorite statement, "May the Light of love and wisdom shine on my path and guide me at all times. May I always act and react in accordance with the highest and best in me. May I fulfill the purpose for which I was born."

I liked using individual problems as a base for developing awareness, understanding, and love. As time went on, I felt more and more the importance of dealing with the *causes* of illness, emotional distress and unhappiness. As I meditated, I became aware of feeling comfortable in the role of teaching values and how to apply spiritual laws to everyday living. And for the rest of my life I felt at home in the arcane world of mystery and knowledge —of love and wisdom.

Chapter IV

The Light Shows the Way

Part 2 — An Attitudinal Healing

As always, I relied upon life's events to show me my next step. I never had long to wait. It is as though the universe knows the ones who rely upon It to show the way, and It never fails. In my personal life, I am often impatient and sometimes I do not attain the best results because of a certain wilfulness or just simple ignorance or ineptitude. But as time goes on, I am learning to be more aware of giving everything over to the Light of higher wisdom and greater impersonal love. The more faithful I am in the daily disciplines, the more life moves forward in a better and more constructive way.

I had learned that physical healings *must* include a deeper understanding of the relative importance of one's emotional and mental attitude toward life, so I was somewhat prepared to deal with the next healing problem that was presented to me. This was the case of a man with an extremely negative attitude toward an unfortunate physical condition.

BOB

I received a phone call from a man who sounded desperately unhappy. After establishing the fact that his neighbor had recommended me to him, we set up an appointment. A few days later, I opened the door to greet a handsome man in his middle 50's. Leaning heavily on a sturdy cane, he hobbled into the room. I could see that each step was painful. One leg was much shorter than the other, which not only impeded his walking, but also distorted his body.

"I hope you can help me," he began. "I am desperate. The doctor made a mess of me. Look what the damn surgeon did." He was speaking so belligerently that for a moment I thought he might include me in his denunciations. As he went on, he became more bitter. "I slipped and fell while mountain climbing and twisted my back. After X-rays were taken, the doctors told me that if I were ever going to walk again I would need back surgery. So what did they do? They finished me off and made a cripple out of me! I'm doomed to live the rest of my life as a cripple!" He paused — "Can you help me? My neighbor, Herbert, told me how much you helped him. Can you give me treatments so that I can walk normally again?"

Magic! He was looking for a miraculous cure — a cure that would add length to a leg shortened and twisted by a spinal injury. But he was an intelligent man and he knew that what he was asking of me was impossible. He knew it and I knew it. So why did he come to see me? As I pondered the question, I intuitively knew the answer.

Bob had to be helped to come to terms with the fact of his condition. He had to learn to accept it and make his peace with it and go on with his life.

I began to question him about his personal life, his way of life, the things he did, his wife and his children.

"My wife is a nervous wreck," he bellowed, "and I'm not making things easy for her since she hears nothing but complaints all day long. I'm always irritable. I hate being a cripple!"

"And your children?"

"Oh, they are good children. My two older sons are now running my business and the youngest one will come into it when he graduates from college, and my daughter might also come into the business. It is *my* business though, and they have to listen to me, toe the mark, and do as I say. Crippled or not, I'm still the boss."

"And how are they doing?" I asked.

"Well, OK, I guess, but the older one has ulcers and the other one has high blood pressure. They're both too young to be sick, but that's the way it is."

The picture was obvious. A whole family wrecked because the head of the family was unable to cope with his unfortunate condition. He seemingly was making everyone close to him suffer because he was suffering. Not uncommon, and quite understandable.

I began talking with him. Did he realize how belligerent he had become? Did he realize that he was undermining the health of his wife and children?

"Look at me! What can I do?" It was almost a cry.

"You can accept your condition as it is. You cannot change what happened in the past, so accept it and go forward. Learn to live with it. Ask yourself each day, 'How can I make life easier for myself, my wife, and my family? How can I guide my sons in the business without harassing them?' Finally, and most importantly, 'What am I supposed to learn from this calamity? How can I conduct myself so that the whole family can be well again?'

"You have two choices: You can let go of your anger and unpleasant ways and become a hero to your family and friends, or you can wallow in bitterness and anger for the rest of your life and continue to make them and yourself miserable. The decision is yours."

There was a silence between us. He was thinking. The idea of being a hero appealed to him—male ego?

"How do I begin?" he said. "Help me."

He had responded to the challenge.

"First of all, take this next week for self-observation. Don't do anything else for this week but listen to your own words and tone of voice. Be aware of your attitude toward your wife and children. Listen—listen to yourself. Don't tell anyone what you are doing and don't try to change anything yet. Just listen. Just be a casual observer, almost as if you were someone else. This process is called objective observation." I asked him to write down the four "don't" rules for self-observation and use them as a guide for his new activity every day: don't justify, don't criticize, don't resent, and don't blame. He wrote them down and we talked about them regularly.

Somewhat intrigued by the instructions, he left in better spirits than when he arrived. His final words were,

"This is most certainly entirely different from what I expected. Thank you."

The following week Bob arrived promptly as we had agreed and immediately launched into his account of the past week.

"I'm really a bastard," were his first words, "much worse than I told you last week. I observed that I blame my wife for every little thing. I constantly ask her to do something for me. I nag. I demand that she wait on me even when it isn't necessary, and I justify my demands by thinking that she has the strength and has nothing better to do than to take care of me. I rant and rave. I yell at my sons constantly, I am critical of everything they do, never praise them because I'm too busy pointing out and correcting their mistakes.

"After four days of observing all of this, I was disgusted with myself. I gave up and became very quiet. For the rest of the week I did a lot of thinking. I don't know how I can stop being such a monster, but I would like to try." He sighed deeply—"I hate being a cripple, and I guess I've been hating my life too. Do you think I can really learn to accept my condition and change my life?"

I told him that I thought he had done a superb job of self-observation, and that it takes many people months to achieve that degree of insight about themselves. I asked him to continue his self-observation and thoughtfulness, and said that the following week we would go deeper into his consciousness and begin the inner work that would implement the changes he wanted to achieve.

Although we had begun each session with a simple

meditation, I had not yet instructed Bob how to include meditation in his daily routine. I did not want to overwhelm him with too much all at one time. But his conscientiousness and his earnest desire to change gave me the signal, a few months later, that he was ready for the whole process—the daily meditations and visualizations that would support his work on changing his attitudes and behavior.

"How about it, Bob," I asked, "are you ready to include meditation in your life? It will take the will to do; it will require patience and perseverance."

"Yes, I want to," Bob replied. "I like the way it relaxes me when we begin our sessions with it. It would be wonderful to feel that good every day."

I pointed out to him that there would be times after meditating when he would feel especially well and uplifted, and there would be other times when he would feel nothing and even feel discouraged. "That is the way it works," I said, "but the 'down' spells are just as important to experience as the 'good' spells. All of it is for your growth and learning—almost like an endurance test. The important thing is that you make a personal vow to meditate every day."

Bob looked thoughtfully at me—"I don't want to let you down, ever."

"No, Bob, not me; you don't make the commitment to me—you make the vow to your own inner self"—I dared—"to the God within you—what I sometimes call *the High Self*."

Bob was startled. In all our discussions, we had never

spoken of God. I could see from his reaction that he was not ready for religious or philosophical concepts. He did not probe further; he did not question. He simply said, "I like that expression—the High Self. It's more comfortable for me." He paused thoughtfully—"And I don't know why."

"Some day we'll go more deeply into the theory of the High Self, the invisible God within and the God without," I answered, "but right now I want to give you a basic meditation that is applicable to your particular situation. We'll begin with the relaxing of the body—something that is important not only for you, but for any beginner in meditation."

We started with simple full breathing—three long deep breaths.

"Breathe in, Bob. Now fill your torso with as much air as it can contain—hold—and breathe out slowly, slowly—relax—let go. Again, breathe in—hold your breath, then breathe out—relax—let go. Resume normal breathing and visualize the air coming through your nostrils. Be aware of the breathing process. With each exhalation feel all tensions flowing out of you, out from every pore of your body, out from the fingertips, out from your toes. With each inhalation, say to yourself, and think it, 'I am breathing in the healing, soothing energy of the universe. The universal goodness is here for my good and It wants me to unite with It. It loves me for submitting myself to Its power. It loves me for recognizing Its desire for my good.' Breathe in—hold—breathe out. Think to yourself, 'Serenity and peace is mine. I am at one with the Universal Goodness—the High Self.' Now remain in this quietude for five minutes, or as long as you can."

We lapsed into the stillness, a silence.

I emerged slowly and watched Bob until he began to stir. I instructed him to come back slowly, very slowly.

"How do you feel?" I asked.

"Wonderful, it would be difficult for me to be angry after such an experience. Will it last?"

"Only if you remain in meditation all day and night, which of course is unrealistic and impossible. But you can use this process to help you establish a more loving relationship with your family; to help you to understand yourself; to be more aware of your actions and reactions. And finally, to change you from a mechanical man drifting through life into an alert, conscious man in charge of his life. And that will last."

"It sounds wonderful," he said, "do you really think I could do it?"

"We'll take it one step at a time, beginning with the daily meditation. After each morning meditation, when you attain a quiet stage, just before returning to your everyday self, you will see yourself as you would like to be. You will be shown how to tap into your ideal self."

Bob was downcast, "I will never be as much as I would like to be because of this awful handicap. I was a good-looking guy before that accident. I was athletic. I was sure of myself and, I guess, a little bit arrogant."

"Your accident," I answered, "is life's way of giving you an opportunity to discover your other fine traits, which can now surface and reveal other aspects of your charac-

ter. It is Life's way of showing you that it is not your physical appearance, crippled or otherwise, that counts, but
how you meet the challenge of this accident that has mu-
tilated your body. You still have your clear-thinking
mind. You have a family who wants to help you. You
have financial means to sustain you comfortably. You
have enormous advantages. You are a lucky man, for by
responding affirmatively to this new challenge you can
learn more and become more of a real man in every sense
of the word. Your so-called accident is Life's odd way of
giving you an opportunity to find the true meaning of
life."

"Is there really a meaning to all of this?" Bob asked
skeptically.

"Someday, Bob, you are going to tell me that you have
found the meaning of it all. But now is your time for self-
rehabilitation through self-examination. You will see
that the method of meditation and visualization will not
be too painful. It will be revealing, but not humiliating."

Bob left taking with him the meditation I had written
down for his daily practice, using the first person "I"
wherever applicable. I advised him to use any abstract
thought of his own, for that which came from his own
creative self was more important for his growth than
what came from me.

I always tell students that it is more important to express themselves in meditation in their own words than
to memorize my words; it is more important to tap one's
own hidden resources than to allow someone else, however well-intentioned, to impose his or her thinking. A
teacher can guide and point the way, but should not in-

terfere with the students' prerogative, the right to think for themselves. My Inner Teacher never commands or imposes, but simply points the way and lets me struggle to find my own strength and learn from my mistakes. Learning by this method is more difficult, but more solid, more creative; it develops independence and self-reliance.

The months flew by and Bob never missed an appointment. He was enjoying his morning meditations and became quite adept. He had the usual complaint of mind-wandering and the subsequent discouragement because of this. I assured him that everyone has that troublesome problem and instructed him to ignore the interruption and simply start over, concentrating on the inhalations and exhalations of the breath.

"Remember, you can always be the controller. If your mind wanders, just gently and quietly resume the breathing. Listen to the breathing, visualize it going in and coming out. Establish yourself as the driver of your vehicle, the boss of your body, mind and emotions. Don't become frustrated. Just remember that you are the parent in control of the child within. You decide what you want, when, and how. Go back to the beginning of your meditation and continue."

In time Bob was able to sit quietly in meditation for about twenty minutes. He was pleased and I was pleased. It was a real accomplishment. He also continued to observe objectively, as he had from the very first week. He reported that some weeks he did well—certainly much better than before we began—but that he sometimes slipped back into the old tyrannical pattern. He observed this aberration objectively and dispassionately as he was instructed to do. He learned not to judge himself harshly.

Bob observed that when he excused his behavior and justified his outbursts, he would at the same time blame the other party in the confrontation, and that in turn resulted in his wallowing in the old self-pity, and then the old habit patterns would return. But now he had changed; he didn't like the old patterns. Those weeks when he had had such regressive moments, he would begin our sessions feeling contrite and discouraged. Oddly enough, it was in those particular sessions that he made his greatest progress. What he saw in himself and didn't like, he was eager to rectify. My faith in his ability to transform the old destructive traits was deeply sincere, and I believe my faith transferred itself to him. It was my High Self relating to his High Self.

As our sessions progressed, I added another meditative method which included imagery. I enjoyed working with the imaging mind, and I think it is a sequential procedure in the meditative process. We had included simple imagery exercises in many of our sessions. For several months Bob was given daily meditations based on the symbols used in the ancient Greek Mystery Schools — the circle, the cross, and the triangle. He was to meditate on each symbol for three minutes, totaling nine minutes.

Although the method is simple, it is difficult to concentrate for three minutes on one object without mind-wandering. Bob had the usual problem with it, but when he imagined himself in front of a huge blackboard with a piece of white chalk in his hand and writing on the board, the process became easier. Sometimes just using the back of one hand to outline each symbol also helps. There are other simple techniques that can be used — anything is permissible.

Bob responded to the imagery sessions very well. But finding the right key to the heart of this particular man came from Bob's earlier reaction to the suggestion of being a hero, and this became a focus of many of our imagery sessions. One day after the usual meditative process, Bob said that he would like to write the word *hero*, H-E-R-O, on his blackboard. I was delighted, as much by the fact that the thought came from him as by the applicability of the idea. He visualized writing the word *hero* on the blackboard and meditated on what he thought a hero would be like. I urged him to keep in meditation and at the same time relate to me just what came to his mind. I recorded the words.

"This guy is great — he is so sure of himself." Silence again. "What a guy. He is so just. I see him as a king of kings, like Solomon. People come to him and he never yells or *belittles* anyone. He is very patient; and so kind."

Silence. Bob continued his meditation in silence. I watched him. He looked so thoughtful and serene. I could see that he enjoyed what he was visualizing. It was a beautiful silence.

Slowly he emerged and opened his eyes. He looked at me and at his surroundings as though to reassure himself that he was where he had started from. I patiently waited for him to speak.

Finally he spoke up: "That was the best meditation I have ever had."

"Tell me about it," I urged.

"King Solomon—that hero was some kind of kingly person," Bob said. "After all the people left I was alone with him" (that had to be the moment he no longer spoke to me). Bob went on: "Something took place between us that I can't describe now, but it was very clear then. I knew inside of me what he was thinking inside of him. It was as though we were communicating, but there were no words. I simply knew him and *oh, how he knew me*. He didn't condemn me even though I knew that he knew what a bastard I was. He just looked at me with so much kindness and love; yes, that's it—love, a kind of love that understands bastards like me and still loves them."

I knew that Bob had had the ultimate experience of the great impersonal love—a "peak" meditation.

He would never be the same again.

And he never was.

Inadvertently Bob had discovered his own Archetypes —the Hero and the Bastard. To further entrench sub-stituting his Hero-Self for the Bastard, we began a series of sessions using imagery to firmly establish that role model in his psyche.

We began with the relaxing meditation. With his eyes closed and completely relaxed, Bob was led in imagery up a flight of stairs. Standing at the top, he was asked to look down at himself and see himself involved in an event of the past week.

"What do you see yourself doing, Bob? Where are you?" I asked.

"I am with my youngest son" (16 years old). "He has just told me he wants to quit high school; he is bored there. I am furious. I am yelling at him. The idiot. What does he think he is doing? I won't allow it." Bob's quiet mood gave way to his angry self.

I interrupted: "The Bastard is having his say. Who are you now?"

"But I am right," Bob continued, "I can't let him quit school at 16. You don't think that I should let him get away with that, do you? Education is very important."

"Look at yourself, Bob. You are very angry."

"You bet I am and rightly so."

"Justifying—isn't that so, Bob?"

"Oh, my God, I am not supposed to justify my reactions even when I know they are right."

"You are speaking from your angry self, Bob. Let's see how to correct that. Breathe in—breathe out—relax—let go. Breathe in—breathe out—relax—let go, again and again. Now in your relaxed state of mind, visualize the Hero. Take your time."

Bob became calm and more thoughtful; in imagery he began to ask questions of his son. With his eyes closed, Bob assumed the Hero role, and the Hero took over. "Why do you want to leave school?" he asked. The boy spoke up, "I want to get into the family business, I've got to leave school; I'm afraid if I wait two more years for my graduation that there will be no place for me. I want to start now."

Bob answered, "But there will always be a place for you, I promise."

"But what if something happens to you, what if you die before I graduate?" The fears were out. Bob, stunned by the revelation, assured his son that he would put the stipulation in writing, he would spell it out word for word. The boy was reassured.

Bob came out of the imagery session glowing with pride and achievement. The first thing he said was, "It works; I see how it works. All I have to do is stop and listen to the other person. I have to listen calmly, and then I will know what to do and how to do it," He became thoughtful again. "That Hero is quite a guy."

"That Hero is you, Bob."

In imagery, Bob had experienced first-hand the results. He couldn't wait to return home and have a fatherly talk with his son, and later reported to me how successfully the Hero had acted. "My son and I are closer than we ever were, we can now talk together about anything and everything. That Hero is a great guy when I let him take control."

Many times after that Bob let the Hero come out of hiding. When the Bastard would act first, Bob would know what to do, and as time went on, the Bastard became less important and his outbursts less frequent. More and more, the Hero acted before the Bastard. It took time, perseverance, and diligence.

Bob learned that he and he alone was responsible for how he experienced his physical condition. His spiritual growth depended on his understanding of the karmic pattern of his accident. He had had a valuable lesson to learn that was more important than a few more years in time doing his same old things in the same old way. His crippled body had led him to someone like me (it could have been any other spiritual teacher) in order to create a new reality and a renewed being. The possibility of looking into his inner being was there from the moment of his birth, but until the so-called accident, there was no desire for change, no desire for growth or for aware-ness. So the accident propelled him into experiencing the meaning of life.

In many of our later sessions, we discussed the High Self—the God within. Towards the end of our year to-gether, he not only did not resist thinking and talking about the God within, but actually seemed to yearn for more connectedness with the inner goodness. How well I understood that yearning! It was my quest, and now it had become Bob's also. We talked for hours on this subject.

It was during those latter months that Bob's medita-tions became more centered, more spiritual. He loved the line of the Psalm, "Be still and know that I am God." But the first time I gave him that quote from the Bible, he said: "It makes me feel funny—sort of uncomfortable. I'm just an ordinary guy, you know, and it seems like such chutzpah, such arrogance, for me to claim to be God."

I confessed that my first reaction to using that as my mantra was similar. I, too, could not say or think it. It wasn't until I thought of the God Self as one with my Higher Self that I understood the God within.

"It is you, Bob, the inner creative High Self within you, and within every being, that is the God Self. We are gods, but until we accept that belief and become one with Him, we are separated from our own goodness and truth. If and when we finally achieve that oneness, then the physical world as we know it will be entirely different. Humanity can create a God-like world—goodness and love can rule the universe."

Bob sighed, "I don't believe I'll live to see it. It seems so remotely idealistic and impossible. Do you really believe man can someday stop all this hate and violence?"

"I hope so. I do believe there is a better future for mankind—a higher and better way of life."

The meetings with Bob were about to be terminated. I never had to be concerned about how to end these sessions. Life had a way of giving me a sign that determined the end of a particular learning process. I had worked with Bob for over a year. We had become good friends. He had made great strides. He had changed his behavior and had learned to accept his painful, crippling condition with courage and a degree of contentment. His wife and children, beneficiaries of his metamorphosis, had often contacted me with expressions of gratitude and delight. The entire family had benefited from his dedicated effort to accept his life's great challenge. He had won the battle. But now the signs showed us that it was time for Bob to "go it alone."

Destiny took over and gave us the signal for the next step. Bob moved to another city, far enough away to make our weekly sessions difficult, but close enough to meet occasionally. It was as it should be; the signs were right—they always are. And Bob the Hero did well on his own. His new-found philosophy appealed to all who would listen, mostly because he himself was a living example of his belief system.

Confined to a wheel chair, Bob lived in a retirement community for twenty-five more years. I saw him frequently during that time. He rarely reverted back to the "Bastard." On the contrary, his patient acceptance of being an invalid, his devotion to his family, his readiness to listen to and comfort friends in need of help, filled his days with purpose. No one knowing him in these later years would have imagined the distance he had come from the bitter, angry, resentful man of the past to the gentle, kind, and wise man of the present. For the rest of his life the "Hero" was his guiding Light.

My last conversation with Bob took place 25 years later, a few weeks before his death. He asked if I would come to visit him in the hospital, as he wanted to tell me about an unusual experience he had just had. I welcomed the chance to see him again.

The next day I went to the hospital. I quietly approached his bed. His eyes were closed, he looked pale and emaciated, but peaceful. He felt my presence and opened his eyes. Now he looked bright and vibrant. He grasped my outstretched hand, "It is all true!" His voice rang out triumphantly.

He then proceeded to tell me what seemed to have been an "out-of-the-body experience." "The nurse had just fixed me for the night, when suddenly I was no longer in my bed; there was something like a clicking sound and I was somewhere else. My body was in the bed, but I was in a very beautiful place, full of joy and light. I felt so happy, so free of all my aches and pains. I was light as a feather. And then people appeared— mostly old friends who had died, all looking so well, young and happy. I wanted to talk with them, but suddenly, in a flash, I was back in this bed again, back in my heavy, painful body. But in those few moments of release from my body, I felt so alive and so well!"

"Why did you come back, Bob, or did you have a choice?"

"I seemed to be pulled down by my wife and children. I wanted so much to tell them how I felt about each one. I wanted them to know about my glorious experience. I wanted everyone to know that no one should be afraid of death."

He continued, "All day yesterday, I thought about our sessions together and how they changed my life. I am so glad that you came today, as I knew you would understand my few moments in another world. Also, I wanted you to know that what you believe in is true — all true. And now I know!"

* * *

The following is a report written by a nurse who was on duty with Bob during his final illness. It was given to me by Bob's daughter, and she has given her permission to include it in this book.

Saddleback Hospital
12–17–79

On Monday 17, 1979, I was called for Private Duty for a Mr. R_____ K_____ in Saddleback Hospital. He had had a bypass operation complicated by Diabetes and a number of other ailments.

A truly lovely man — so gentle and kind. So quick to speak well of everyone. A good family man, who dearly loved his family.

My first day passed with normal duties, more than the usual because the man had been given a medication which he could not tolerate and it made his mind practically in-active.

My second day he was coming out from under the medication and could coordinate his thoughts and make sense. He seemed to be coming back from a long journey. He had had much company this day and he was so wound up he could not sleep even tho he'd been given medication. He needed to test his memory like a person who has been away for a while and has come back to another area.

Noting the man needed to talk, I pulled a chair up to bedside, rubbed his back and arms while he went on and on. He asked me about my husband and if I was married, and I told him I had been married for 34 years when I lost my husband, a flyer in the airforce, with diabetes — my husband had had four amputations plus 3 strokes. Mr. K_____ said, "Oh, you have fortitude and you've been badly hurt." Then he said, "He can see you, I know. I've been over there, they did question me too, it was beautiful and I wanted to stay, but my wife needs me here for a while." He said, "I've seen the Celestial body and I only crossed thru; it's beautiful, no pain. I have much pain here but I suffer this for my family. We were all put here to do good — if only people could see this; they never do, until it's too late. We are supposed to work together."

Then he started thanking all the people that had helped him, been good to him, as far back as he could remember. Then he said, "I've done my daughter Gladys a very bad injustice. I must make it up to my beautiful daughter." He said, "I did not think she was good enough for my son-in-law. Now I can see I am so wrong."

Then he thanked people for a while, blessed them, then said to me, "You will have it easier now; I can see it's going to be alright for you." I felt eerie as if my flesh were crawling because it was as if the man was not human anymore. He touched my shoulder with his hand and it felt as if it almost glowed—a very remarkable experience.

I feel as if the man went beyond and was called back for a purpose. (Nothing seems to truly hurt him too bad. The medication nurse gives him a blood thinner shot into his stomach each 8 hours, and as tender as one's stomach is, he does not flinch.)

He then spoke of his youngest son; he said, "He was my medicine, he will carry on everything for peace to man that he can." He called him his youngest son in Hebrew, and some more words in Hebrew. He also said to the nurse, "I have to tell my family some things when I can; I am supposed to be secret on these matters now." He said, "There was a whole body of people who questioned me." I said, "Could you say what about?" He said, "No, they were testing me. I passed the test, they know what I must do." He also spoke of a Jewish daughter-in-law as an angel. Then he lapsed into talk with people whom he said he had not seen for several years.

He told me, "I saw all my old friends there, that I'd not seen for years. Now I know why I was so surprised to see them." "But I've got a lot of friends here, or I did have — no, I mean I do have; is my memory correct?" I assured him it was.

I truly believe the man has seen a Celestial being and has been touched and returned here for a purpose — I cannot guess what. However, he keeps repeating, "We must be better to each other; we also must work for a Common Cause, an end to all this turmoil." "Eleanor," he said, "you're a good person; it's sad we have so few good people left."

He also, for past 3 days, has spoken of an Anabelle, saying he was so much richer for having known her, and God bless her, and on and on. He gave me a blessing. He said, "I am concentrating on you being able to live a good life here, until you cross over." I thanked him.

A life well lived, my friend Bob, until we meet again — blessings.

Chapter V

Healing the Past

Part 1

How man uses the span of time allotted to him on the planet earth determines the course of his life and the course of history. Time can be an enemy or a friend. The passage of time can either heal the sorrow of losing a loved one, or it can serve to deepen old hurts. We can use time productively, or we can waste time idly. The more I delved into the important role time plays in all our lives, the more I found others who were equally as enthralled by the subject. The famous scientist Stephen Hawking *(A Brief History of Time)* and the scientist-novelist Alan Lightman *(Einstein's Dreams)* were also writing about time, and their books were on the best-seller list. And the most widely read book of all, The Holy Bible, contains the famous verse about Time from Ecclesiastes:

A time to laugh and a time to cry,
A time to live and a time to die.

In the long history of human development, time has always played an important role. Before recorded time, our ancestors depended on the activity of the sun and the moon to regulate their daily lives. They worshipped the planets, and lived according to their activities. Down through the ages, time has continued to regulate daily living. We all depend on our watches. At a set time we awake, go to school, to work, doctors' appointments, breakfast, lunch, dinner, rest, sleep. We celebrate our birthdays and our holidays at certain times of the year.

We program ourselves constantly, still living as our ancestors did by the dictates of the rising and setting sun, whose movements are precise and dependable. The sun never fails. It never disappoints. For many of us it represents security and is scientific proof that there is some kind of Supreme Intelligence ruling the universe. There is yesterday, today, tomorrow, night following day, and on and on — a slow march from birth to youth, old age and death. The planet Earth is our home, the movement of the sun is our security blanket. We live by the dictates of time as slaves marching to the beat of its drum. Anchored by time and gravity to our planet, our home, we journey on and on from yesterday — today — tomorrow, our security dependent upon our inherited adherence to the laws of the universe.

But the orderliness of the physical, objective world does not extend to our emotions. The violent nature of man can explode any time, anywhere, as it now has, much to our discomfort. As I continued my meditation on the meaning of time, it seemed important to understand the volatile, unreliable nature of the emotional side of man. Our emotions don't make set appointments to be angry. They are not bound by the rules and regulations of time. They can strike out quickly and cunningly, bypassing the reasoning side of man; and without the restraints of the intellect, man's negative, destructive nature may run wildly downhill. Time then no longer serves the rule of order, but succumbs to the rule of entropy.

We know that a harmful event of the past can attack an unprotected child and plant itself firmly in the unconscious, beyond the reach of the rational mind. The wounded child of the past then lives on and on, torturing the adult with unceasing fears and anxieties, made more powerful and destructive by time. Even when the adult later learns about the traumas of his childhood, the knowledge alone does not save him from the continuing downward spiral, unless he is willing to deal with the early causes.

A man of sixty, who had been affected all his life by an emotionally charged incident in his very early years, said to me, "Of course I know about it. Everybody has since told me, and I guess it is true. So what? I don't think that incident is the cause of my sleepless nights, my fears and my anxieties."

Others have told me, "I know I was abused in my childhood. I don't remember the specifics, but I know it to be true. I was an unhappy child. I never had a so-called carefree childhood. At the age of seventeen, I realized that I was never happy, nor did I expect to be."

It was while meditating on statements of this kind, that I realized that there was a missing link, and that something further had to be done in order to repair the damage of the psyche of the very young. A remedy seemed elusive. As customary, I waited for the Inner Teacher to give me answers — to show the way.

HELEN AND CHARLES

I didn't have long to wait. A most unexpected call came from Ruth, a former client whom I hadn't seen in a long time. She asked if I would see her and a couple of friends who were in trouble and needed help. I loved Ruth, and greatly admired how she had worked out her life's difficulties. We agreed on a time.

One of the most unusual experiences of my life was to come out of that meeting.

Ruth and her two friends, Nan and Helen, arrived promptly. They had come some distance, mainly to give comfort to Nan who had recently lost her eighteen-year-old son. We prayed and meditated and talked about death. It seemed to help Nan just to be able to talk with understanding friends about the tragedy. They were about to leave, when I turned to Helen and asked how life was treating her.

Looking sad, Helen sighed as she said, "I have a very serious problem, which I have lived with for a very long time. But now I admit it is getting me down, wearing me out, so that when Ruth asked me to join her, I jumped at the opportunity. I wanted so much to see you."

I invited Helen to tell me her problem.

"It's my husband," she said tearfully. "He has been severely depressed for as long as I can remember. But the last two or three years, he has become so much worse, and increasingly difficult to live with."

"How is he worse now? Describe his daily life."

"He just sits around the house all day long. He eats and sleeps and just sits. He won't see a doctor. He won't take the pills that were prescribed. He won't do anything. He is terribly depressed."

"Helen, this is serious. And awful for you. How do you endure it?"

"I have my studies. I attend group meetings. I do the usual chores and see a few friends. If it weren't for my belief in God and my spiritual pursuits, I could not survive. But I must admit, I am exhausted."

"Of course," I said. "It is too much for any one person to live with. And the bandaids in the form of activities can't help forever. By any chance, Helen do you know what might have caused his breakdown?"

"Oh yes, I do know, because he has talked about it many times. It goes back many years to an incident which occurred when he was seven years old. Up to that age, he described himself as a happy child, strongly attached to his father, with whom he had a very special relationship, made more significant by the fact that his mother was coldly distant. However, the close relationship with his father changed when his father became ill with a terminal disease. When the end was approaching, his father's deteriorating body and speech frightened him. He could no longer bear to be with him. Above all, the little boy had a terrible fear of death. As time went on, he became increasingly more frightened and, instead of helping him to understand his fears, his mother scolded him, punished him and tried to force him to spend time with his father. The more his father's appearance deteriorated, and the more his mother insisted, the more terrified Charles became. In spite of all his protestations, as the end approached, his mother urged him to go once more into the room and kiss his father goodbye. They battled. He refused. The father died."

Helen paused as she related the events. She continued, "So Charles not only suffered from the grief of losing his father, but was also consumed by guilt. Long after his father's death, the mother constantly reminded him of his failure to comfort his dying father. She never let up! Even on *her* deathbed, she reminded him — 'You never kissed your father goodbye.'

"For years Charles has carried this burden of loss, grief and guilt. He often dreams about it, and sometimes wakes up screaming. And part of his burden is his terrible fear of death."

Here was a case where knowledge of the past event did not help to go beyond the pain. Charles never forgave himself. And now, approaching his seventieth birthday, the struggle of that seven-year-old was still going on, paralyzing the 69-year-old man. The frightened and guilt-ridden child of the past lived on and finally took control of the physical, emotional and mental body of the adult. Charles the adult was wrecked by a past happening that was never resolved. The child and the adult were victimized by the continual taunting and destructive attitude of the mother. During her life, and beyond, the mother unwittingly was destroying her son.

After Helen had finished telling us about her husband's condition, our little group was quiet, each of us with our own thoughts. I said that I believed Helen and I had to do a special meditation, that the other two could help enormously by relaxing and meditating with us. I led the group in a meditation. At that moment I was not thinking about a healing for Charles; I was merely trying to find a way to ease Helen's burden. We all relaxed, getting more and more quiet, sinking deeper into that other dimension of love and wisdom. The thoughts and impressions were coming quickly.

Inwardly I asked for help. In a flash, the answer came: heal the past. At the same moment, I had the first inkling that this was not going to produce a symbol or thought for Helen's daily meditation, but something far more significant. "Heal the past"—Time! The thoughts, the impressions, were coming quickly, and at the same moment I became aware of a pink glow enveloping a beautiful, overpowering female Presence. I sank deeper and deeper into the inner self. The thoughts and impressions came faster and faster, more and more specific.

I had to tell Helen what I was experiencing before going further into the deeper inner self. I knew that the Presence was going to help us, but I had to be in that other dimension and my own at the same time— simultaneously in two worlds—the world of creativity and the world of materiality. I seemed to be flooded with new thoughts and ideas and, at the same time, I had to stay grounded enough to relay the messages to Helen. As always, it all came in pictures.

I began to speak. "We are to go back sixty-three years in time, Helen. *You* are going to assume the role of the child's mother. You are the surrogate mother, so to speak. You are going to comfort the frightened little boy—tell him how much you love him—tell him you understand his fear of going into the room of his dying father. Comfort the child, and tell him it is difficult for you, too. Tell him it is OK, and that he doesn't have to go into the dying father's room.

Helen responds to the instructions. She speaks. "I am picking him up and holding him in my lap. 'Don't worry, Charles. It's OK. You don't have to go into that room. Dad knows you love him, just as he loves you. He understands your fear. Don't cry. Just remember him with love. You gave him great comfort and joy all the years of your life. That was important.'"

Helen then reported. "It seems like he's telling me how frightened he is." She, too, was deeply moved.

"Keep on, Helen. Keep reassuring him, and tell him whatever he does, his father understands. He doesn't have to do anything but just love him." I was speaking to Helen, and at the same time I was receiving instructions from that source beyond myself.

Helen said, "I am rocking him, comforting him. He seems to be calmer now, relaxed."

"Good. Continue to rock him, for I feel at this moment the universality of all mothers."

We were silent as we absorbed the reality of the love surrounding us. It was overpowering, and I spoke with great difficulty as the power of the mother image overwhelmed me. I was getting more imagery messages than I could relate. But later I realized that the important thing to remember was the almost untranslatable feeling of love that came from the Archetypal Mother—a love that filled the whole room with the power of its beauty; a love for this little boy, Charles, and for all children in emotional distress. And yes, forgiveness. We must remember to include the real mother. Even on the other side of life, she yearns for forgiveness.

Helen continued, telling the seven-year-old child that it is not necessary to kiss his father goodbye, that he needs only to say to his father, "I love you, Dad. I am too frightened to look at you and kiss you now, but I love you. And mother tells me it's OK to be scared, and that you understand, and that the love between us is the most important thing of all. She says a lot of people are frightened. And I don't have to think about anything else but my love for you."

We meditated silently for quite some time. I reviewed in my mind the session—the little boy being comforted now by a mother who understood the fear of a seven-year-old. Going back in time, we seemed to be directed to play the same scene of the past with the same cast of characters, the same conditions, but with changed attitudes, changed words, changed meanings. By replacing a harsh, cruel moment with kind, comforting words of understanding and love, the destructiveness of that moment was nullified.

The healing session and our meditations were over. I looked up and saw a pink glow reflected on Helen's face. All of us were greatly moved.

Helen asked, "Should I tell Charles what we just did for him?"

I answered, "No, I think it is better to say nothing."

In the beginning it is wiser just to let the creative process take its own course and take the cue from further developments. The results are not in my hands, not in Helen's, but only in the hands of the Supreme Mother. A higher power inspired the moment, showed us the way, and re-created the past. In some unknown way, that higher power had taken control. Whatever the result, *IT* is responsible.

After the group left, I sat quietly for a long time, thinking again about the nature of time as it involved man's emotional nature. I realized that I was being shown that by moving time back into the past of the adult, and constructively dealing with the emotions at the moment of the initial blow to the psyche, time in retrograde became the tool of the creative power of love. The conditions of time change when we no longer live by the linear rules of our planet. The rules change when, without gravitation, objects move in unrestricted space. The rules change when past and future become interchangeable. By virtue of their ephemeral nature, the emotional and mental states of man are governed by the same conditions as man in outer space. Emotionally, mentally, and spiritually we have no boundaries.

A few days later Helen called.

"You won't believe what I am going to tell you." She spoke quietly. "When I came home after our session, Charles greeted me at the door. He looked wonderful, as I haven't seen him in a very long time. His first words were incredible. I was dumbfounded—my knees buckled under me, and my eyes filled with tears.

" 'While you were away I was just sitting here quietly

when suddenly I felt the presence of my mother. You know, I never had any love for my mother. Then in a few moments she was gone. It all happened so quickly. I now have such a remarkable sense of relief. I think I'm released from her! I can't understand it, but I feel happier than I have felt for a very long time!' He looked at me and said, 'You find it hard to believe, too. You look so stunned.' "

In spite of my many experiences of such so-called miracles, I was speechless. Helen and I figured that Charles must have received the release at the same time that we were deeply immersed in the glow of our imaging meditation.

Helen continued, "I waited a few days before calling you, because I wanted to be sure, and I was too much in awe of the whole thing to talk about it. But I have more to report. Even if he hadn't used the word 'release,' his actions are now that of a free man."

I felt a chill run down my spine. This good man of almost seventy was going to be able to live his last years in freedom. A great burden had been lifted from him. A blessing for Helen. I thanked God.

Helen went on, "He helps in the house, and he wants to share in all the chores. He even asked if he could do the marketing. It has been a long time since he has wanted to do anything."

Later in the same week, Helen called again to further report on Charles' progress. Her voice sounded so happy: "We are going to visit our children on Sunday. We haven't done that in a very long time. And something else. We are going to San Diego for a weekend with a couple of our friends." Her voice rang out, "It is so good to be able to live a normal life again!"

Together we rejoiced. Together we said our prayer and gave thanks to the Supreme Being—the Eternal Mother.

* * *

The unexpected appearance of the angelic being of Mother Love had a profound effect on me. I realized that all my theorizing about Time—all the meditations on Time—came to a climax with the advent of the Universal Mother. In that extraordinary session, she had shown us how to repair the damage done by unknowing, and often cruel, mothers. She had shown us how, by erasing the past, the psyche of the unprotected child could be healed and, by substituting a loving, compassionate mother, the image of positive motherhood could be established and universally known.

On a personal level, I felt that I had a transfusion of the Mother Love, which nurtured and healed my old feelings of childhood neglect and rejection. More strangely, from that time on, I felt connected with others needing the power of Mother Love to heal the sorrow of abuse by their mothers.

But most importantly, a sense of the presence of the Angelic Being of Love never left me, a connectedness that seems to be strengthened as time goes on.

Chapter VI

Healing the Past

Part 2

It wasn't long before another case of early childhood trauma came my way—the result of an unexpected visit from Betty, a student for many years. I told her about the recent amazing experience with Helen and Charles. She listened intently, and, after a thoughtful silence, said that she had come to see me at this particular time because she was so deeply troubled about her husband, Sam.

"There are times," she said, "when he acts as though he hates me, and I cry myself to sleep. More often than not, I fight back and don't let him get away with it. So we quarrel a lot, privately and publicly. It is demeaning and painful for me."

Many times in the past, Betty had confided to me how Sam constantly insulted her, was always criticizing and "putting her down." Whenever I asked her why she remained in the marriage, she invariably gave me several good reasons. "First of all," she said, "the time you and I have spent together studying metaphysics, translating dreams, working with imagery, helped me value myself in spite of his derogatory attitude towards me. And secondly, as I always told you, he is good. He can be kind and generous. He loves to help other people, and he is charitable and honest. I believe he is devoted to me, even though his feelings are deeply buried. Yet he acts as though he can't stand being with me. As time goes on, it is getting more and more unbearable. But I will not leave him, nor has he ever indicated that he would want me to. Most importantly, long ago, I came to believe that he is my karma.

"You know," Betty continued, "he used to treat his mother the same way he treats me. He seemed to have no respect for her, was always belittling her and expressing anger toward her. She told me once that she felt she deserved to be punished by him because of the terrible ordeal she had put him through in his infancy and, for the same reason, she had rarely disciplined him as a child. Perhaps that's why he never respected her. Knowing how a man transfers his feelings for his mother to his wife, I understand why he treats me like he does, but it is spoiling our marriage."

I asked Betty if she knew what the ordeal was that Sam had experienced as an infant.

"Yes," Betty replied. "Tanya, Sam's mother, told me about it a few years before she died."

The following is Tanya's story as she told it to her daughter-in-law, Betty:

Jacob and I were in our twenties. I had just given birth to Samuel, when Jacob was conscripted and forced to join the Russian army. The Russian Armed Forces lived under very harsh conditions, but for Jewish men, victims of terrible anti-Semitism, it was unbearable. Many did not survive, and the few who returned brought back tales of violence, depravation and torture. It was considered right for Christian Russians to mistreat the Jews. So a call to service for Jewish men was equivalent to a call to death.

When Jacob was conscripted, we immediately planned to join the hoardes of Jews who were trying to escape from the pogroms and torture of anti-Semitic Russia. At that time, there was a way to leave the country if you had enough money.

We sold all our belongings, taking only the bare necessities with us. As was customary, we bribed the official in charge and were told to join up with a small group of other Jews, all of us meeting at a designated place at the border.

When Jacob and I, carrying our infant son, arrived at that place, the other members of the group protested our joining them. They insisted that we couldn't stay, because our baby would cry and give away the hiding place. Some of them had left their babies with relatives, rather than jeopardize their lives and the lives of others. So it was upsetting to them that we dared bring our baby, while they had left theirs behind. But we pleaded with them that we couldn't go back, because Jacob was on the wanted list, and as a deserter, he would be tortured and put to certain death.

In desperation, I promised that I would, and could, stifle my baby's cries. Showing them how I would do it, I pulled out a coarse cloth from our pack and stuffed it into my baby's mouth and gagged him. The group looked on in horror, but they no longer had an excuse to send us away.

As I bound little Samuel's mouth, the look in that 10-week-old baby's eyes was terrible. I cried and cried, but I had to do it, or it was the end for all three of us. It took several days before we were given the signal for our escape, and all that time, I kept the gag on that poor, suffering baby. It was awful! He suffered so much! It was terrible for me, terrible!

As Betty finished the story she was in tears, just as Tanya had cried fresh tears of anguish when she told the story to Betty. But neither Betty nor her mother-in-law had ever connected Sam's constant anger with the ordeal suffered in his infancy.

It was interesting to me that over all our years of friendship and study, Betty had never told me this significant episode of Sam's infancy. Whenever we discussed his incorrigible behavior, we concluded that he needed psychological counseling, which he adamantly refused to consider. Up to this moment, Betty might not even have thought to tell me the story, if I hadn't given her a detailed report of the momentous meeting with Helen, and her husband's subsequent healing. Now, she had a doubtful moment of hope.

"I don't suppose Sam could be considered a candidate for that kind of healing?" Betty asked sceptically. "He was only an infant, so of course he doesn't remember anything. And now, at almost 70 years of age, he is rooted in his behavior patterns. Do you think it is too late; is it possible that *anything* could help him now?"

Although concerned about her doubts, I hastened to tell her that all memory is buried in the psyche going back to the time of birth, and that although Sam doesn't consciously remember, his soul does.

I silently wished she could have been present when the power of the Universal Mother pervaded the room! Her mystical tendencies would have responded. But now she had to rely on the evidence I had given her. However, she trusted me and definitely wanted to try the new process. She understood and willingly accepted the role of the surrogate mother.

And so, once again, I joined with a substitute mother in meditation to prepare for remedying an unusual event that occurred nearly seventy years ago. We did our usual breathing exercise, this time using the count-down method, gradually slipping deeper, until the atmosphere around us became heavy with the silence.

Later Betty reported, "I felt as though the deeper I went, the closer I became connected with that frightened, huddled group of people at the Polish border. I heard your voice guiding me in imagery as I bent down to take that poor, silent, suffering baby in my arms."

(That was the moment that Betty broke down and wept.) Through her tears, her voice breaking, she sobbed words of comfort and love to the tortured infant. I could barely hear her as she explained to him why she, as the mother, had to gag him. Betty continued, "I can't stand making you suffer. I am suffering, too. But we will be destroyed if you cry or make any sound at all. I am doing this awful thing because I love you. I want you to have a long life because I love you. I love you. I love you." She rocked, cuddled and comforted him. Tears flowing, she sang to him, holding him close to her for a long time.

I remained in meditation and prayer until I knew she had completed her mission. Quietly, we returned to the present, both of us exhausted from the emotional stress of reliving the emotional pain and suffering of the past. We concluded by reciting our usual prayer of gratitude.

Hopefully, by erasing the past, bringing a healing prayer of love to the present, creating a future filled with love and trust, the adult Sam would be healed.

Hopefully, by releasing the torment from the soul of a long-suffering Tanya, she would find her peace.

* * *

Several days later I heard from Betty. "The change in Sam is incredible! I can't get used to it! Will it last?"

"I don't know, we have to give it more time. Meantime don't forget your role of the nurturing Mother."

As time went on Sam often vacillated and wavered between his old and new pattern of behavior, but on the whole Betty was encouraged.

At our next session Betty admitted that "in all honesty

even when he reverts, it is never as bad as it used to be. In general, there is not only a change in his attitude toward me, but also in his attitude toward members of the family, which has always been a problem."

"How?" I asked.

"He is far more tolerant and understanding. Even if nothing else had improved, that difference is an important factor in our lives. In those moments I find it easier to enact my role of the nurturing Mother."

Betty asked about the other cases I was involved with.

"That is a good question. Several have been remarkably remedied. Others have been like yours, a breakthrough mostly in relationships. In all cases a door has been opened, an opening created. I hope some day soon that you will be able to talk to Sam and tell him about the trauma suffered in his infancy, how it affected his whole life, and how instrumental you were in bringing about a healing for him."

"I would love to be able to tell him about my involvement in spiritual practice. I would like him to know how much it helped me to understand myself and how I prayed that one day he, too, would become involved."

"In time your prayers could be answered," I assured Betty. "A healing of this magnitude coming from the spiritual dimension with so much love and power must eventually be given the homage it deserves. A mystical healing is not a random gift to be lightly received and unacknowledged, but a blessing bestowed upon the recipients by the beneficent power of the Universe. It is essential that Sam and the others be told the truth and given the opportunity to thank the Giver."

As time went on, Sam continued to improve to the

point where some months later Betty breathlessly declared, "We are having a wonderful time together! The good moments have become habitual! Never in my wildest dreams did I imagine that he could change so dramatically. It's a miracle!"

And now, ten months later, she no longer has doubts.

Chapter VII

Connectedness

I was just getting accustomed to a deeper understanding of the events of the past nine months when two other unusual healings occurred which further demonstrated our connection with each other and with the healing energy of the universe. Every method I ever knew and used in the past came into play—distant healing, imagery, and thought-transference, all with an added demonstration of a different and unusual way the power of the Light communicated with me.

It all started with the telephone call from Ellie, a devoted student and my dear friend for many years. Once more the mystical and the practical combined to demonstrate another unusual healing experience. Obviously, Ellie was in trouble. Her voice over the phone was barely audible.

"I hate to bother you," she whispered, "but I know you would want to know. I climbed on a chair yesterday to get a jar from a high shelf and lost my balance. I fell off and couldn't move." With great difficulty she continued telling me how her neighbors heard her scream, called the ambulance and rushed her to the hospital. The X-rays revealed that she had fractured three ribs and the only remedy was complete immobility.

"The pain is awful," she continued, "and if I dare move, I scream; not even pain-killers help."

She wasn't exaggerating, as it is common knowledge that fractured ribs heal very slowly, especially for women of Ellie's age — the bones in an 82-year-old are fragile. While listening to Ellie, I suddenly became aware of a tingling sensation in my hands similar to, but with stronger vibrations than, the feeling I get when I place my hands on a physical body of a person in great pain. But Ellie was 60 miles away, our only connection the telephone. The tingling vibrations became stronger and more urgent. Suddenly I got the message and realized what I was supposed to do.

I spoke to Ellie, "I am going to give you a healing meditation right now." Nothing I ever said surprised Ellie — she was always so trusting. "Get as comfortable as you can and keep your ear close to the phone." I began the relaxing meditation, very familiar to Ellie, of breathing and concentrating on the breath. I could hear her quiet breathing, doing the best she could with fractured ribs. The rest took place in imagery. With my hands vibrating, I visualized Ellie standing directly in front of me. In imagery, I placed my tingling vibrating right hand on her rib cage and my left hand directly opposite on her back. Immediately, the vibrating sensation became stronger. I felt no pain — only an electrifying vibration. I remained in that position for what seemed like a long time but was probably about five to ten mintues. I could hear Ellie's slow, labored breathing over the phone as we gave ourselves over to the healing Light. When the vibrations ceased and the healing session was over, I told Ellie to try to sleep and that I would call back later. The next day when I checked with Ellie, the pain had decreased considerably. On the third day when I checked, she excitedly exclaimed that on the scale of one to ten she was now five. Again, in imagery, I put my hands on her rib cage as directed by the vibrations which alerted me that it was time for another healing. Six days after the fall, Ellie happily reported feeling free of pain and was no longer confined to her bed. She reported to her physician, and the X-ray showed a complete healing.

Ellie and I rejoiced and gave credit to the angelic force that had inspired me and was responsible for the healing. It was our custom to meditate and pray to that healing Light which so miraculously did the healing.

* * *

New experiences seem to come in multiples, one immediately following the other. I had just finished speaking to Ellie, when another friend in trouble called.

Jay had no way of knowing what I had just experienced and was not asking for a healing. He simply phoned to break an appointment. I barely recognized his voice as he told me the reason for the cancellation.

"I never thought that anything could be so excruciatingly painful." I could hear in his voice the effort it took to explain his condition to me. "What is the matter, Jay?" I asked.

"I was operated on five days ago for hemorrhoids and

I am not healing very well. It seems to get worse every day. The surgeon says there is nothing he can do, nature and time will eventually heal the condition. But I am in terrible pain." His suffering was in his voice.

I offered the customary words of sympathy and was about to terminate the conversation when again the tingling in my hands began and in a matter of seconds my body was vibrating just as it had a week ago while talking to Ellie.

"Just a moment, Jay," I spoke up, "hold on, I am going to give you a healing treatment over the phone. Listen to my voice, follow the instructions and don't hang up until I tell you to. There will be many moments of silence but keep the connection. I will let you know when the healing session is completed."

I began, "Relax, breathe in, breathe out, relax." Over and over again I repeated the simple relaxing/breathing exercise which I had done hundreds of times. I continued until I could hear his breathing getting slower and slower, quieter and quieter. When Jay seemed reasonably relaxed, I began the imagery session. Visualizing Jay's buttocks on my right hand and my left hand opposite, sitting in my living room with the intimate parts of his body between my two hands, I could do an imagery that would have been embarrassing and uncomfortable on the physical material level. Jay had no idea what I was doing. Again, as in Ellie's case, I held my vibrating hands in that intimate position until the vibrating slowed down. It must have taken about ten minutes. The first healing session was over.

I broke the silence and asked one simple question: "How do you feel?"

"Wonderful," the sleepy voice replied.

"Good. Relax; I will call you tomorrow." I called twice more that week. Each time, *on signal*, I repeated the imagery session. The sixth day when I called, an excited, happy Jay answered the phone. "What did you do? I can't believe what has happened. A few days ago, I was in agony and now I am completely free of all pain. I am a little weak, but that's all. I can never thank you enough!"

I told him to allow nature to complete the job, to rest, and return to work after the next doctor's appointment, which was scheduled the following week. The rest is history—a repeat of Ellie's experience. After the surgeon's astounded "Wow, what a beautiful healing!" Jay was dismissed.

As always, I am completely in awe of the healing power. It has been forty years since my first healing experience (my husband's ulcer). But these last healings of Ellie and Jay, when all I did was respond to a signal and interpret its meaning, was not only startling evidence of the power of the Light, but also an extraordinary way of transmitting that power.

I thanked the Inner Teacher for simplifying my role, easing my misgivings and relieving my recent concern of using an aging body for transmitting energy. But I was shown, in no uncertain terms, what I should do. I didn't have to decide who, what, or when to heal; I merely had to respond to the vibrational signals—the healing channel was opened when I felt the tingling electricity in my hands!

I have always accepted the healing experiences as a demonstration of the power of the healing Light. I always knew that I was just an instrument of conveyance, and that my spiritual, mental and physical bodies were being used by that power of Light, the healing Angels, which I believed in, and which I trusted. I often felt that the recipients weren't nearly as grateful as I. But being on the receiving end, how could they know the joy of being connected with the Spiritual Kingdom? How did I fail to make that connection apparent to them? How much longer would my aging mind and body be used? These were some of the questions which absorbed me during my morning meditations.

And then came the great California Northridge earthquake, a few miles from where I lived in Westwood. If I had deliberately planned to leave my home and go to the safest place in Westwood, I couldn't have done a better job. It would be understandable if I could confess that I had a psychic warning, or an intuitive feeling that an earthquake was imminent. But that would be totally untrue and dishonest. Instead, because of an earlier-in-the-day asthmatic attack, I called my doctor on the staff at UCLA. It was very late in the evening and I hated to disturb him. Doing so was contrary to my usual behavior. Nevertheless, I followed his instructions as he arranged for my admission to the emergency room. I did not think I was critically ill, and yet I couldn't stop my actions as I hurriedly packed my things.

At midnight I was admitted, and at 4:30 in the morning when the earthquake hit, I was in one of the most earthquake-proof buildings in Los Angeles. It creaked and swayed, roared and groaned, but nothing in my hospital room budged an inch. But my bedroom at home was a disaster. A large TV set and stand slid across the room and landed at the foot of my bed; a bookcase emptied itself on the other side of my bed; a lamp fell on the pillow where my head would have been. Broken bric-a-brac and glass were scattered everywhere. I would have been in total darkness, eight stories high, traumatized or hurt.

But in the hospital room, the auxiliary light never went out. Seconds following the aftershock someone of the staff dashed into my room to check on me. It was comforting and reassuring. From beginning to end, I was efficiently and thoughtfully cared for. Beyond coincidence, it was awesome. Everyone called it lucky — luck?! I thanked God for the blessing of having been in the right place at the right time.

I didn't take the above incident lightly. I knew that I had been saved by something beyond my control, something greater than I — something from the same source as the signals prior to the healings of Ellie and Jay.

All these events were milestones in my life, not only because of the last two healings, but mainly because I became more aware of the closeness of the Angelic Kingdom. My early experiences 40 years ago in physical healings had opened up the doors of learning about the spiritual world — the physical manifestations of the power of the Light. And now, 40 years later, it took spiritual healings again to demonstrate a new and intimate way in which the Light could communicate directly with me. The two healings via the telephone were extraordinary evidence of my response to a vibratory signal from an area beyond my usual concepts and knowledge. I was more in awe and impressed by the way I received the communication than I was by the actual healing! I was impressed by the availability of the spiritual dimensions, and that the Angels of love and healing were close by and could contact us. To heal and be healed by an invisible power is a *blessing*!

Even though I had been the human transmitter of this energy, I personally am not in any way unusual, nor is the energy surrounding all of us unusual. Since time began, there have always been human beings who can heal, and there have always been fields of energy surrounding us emanating from the plant, animal and human kingdoms, and to a lesser degree, the mineral. Energy fields are universal and a major means of communicating on the subliminal levels. All sentient beings seem to communicate from their own energy field. As I was meditating at dusk one day, I was absorbed listening to a bird singing its evening song. All at once, I felt the bird's throat in mine — we were singing together! A marvelous sense of oneness overpowered me, as the bird and I became so intimately connected!

It is when the invisible dimension gives evidence of its existence that we begin to accept its presence and availability. Even the scientists give credibility to the smallest invisible particle, the quark, based on its "trail of evidence." Admitting that the quark cannot be microscopically seen or measured, scientists accept its part in the building of the universe, based only on evidence. The mystic gives credit to an invisible Universe also based on evidence.

Feeling the connection of all of us to each other, and to the world around us, is the beginning of accepting the all-pervasive power of the spiritual energy.

Chapter VIII

Acknowledging the Light

I am certain that everything I experienced of an unusual and esoteric nature in the past forty years has been due to the influence of the Light. From the moment I was absorbed in the Light, and became one with it, I became a different person. My attitudes changed, the direction of my life changed, and the spectacular events that would have been strange to the old me were understandable to the new me. Although always in awe of the miraculous and unexpected, I completely accepted the extraordinary healings as something innately characteristic of the power of the Light.

The spectacular healing *is* impressive, and proves the power of the Light, but the phenomenal has a way of overshadowing the underlying purpose of such an experience. For the main purpose (and to my way of thinking, the only purpose) of these phenomena, is to bring into our awareness the knowledge that there is a higher self and a greater power that is constantly available to manifest in our daily lives. It does not always come in a dramatic way, but it is up to each one of us to be aware of, and open to, the possibility that such an experience may enter our ordinary lives at any moment. I have known many people who live serenely aware that there is something greater than they are, something beyond the five senses, that influences their thoughts and feelings. They have not experienced any breathtaking phenomena, but life to them is an adventure into the unknown, a discovery of the intuitive self, an awakening of the creative facets of their minds.

The Light does not have to prove anything. *It just is.* And those who are open to it know and are blessed. I was recently asked if all the unusual healing experiences I described would be accepted as *proof* that there is such a thing as spiritual healings. "You know," the scientist challenged me, "a few successes do not scientifically prove anything. You have to conduct experiments under laboratory conditions to prove the soundness of any method." I pointed out to him that it is not my purpose to prove anything to the scientific world. I am not interested in trying to convince scientists and unbelievers. I have merely stated my case as it happened. Those whose lives have been enhanced have proof enough that following the path of the Light gives them more wisdom, further access to the creative process, inspiration and fulfillment. They need no other proof.

* * *

After the advent of the Mother Figure, new people from all walks of life began seeking me out, as though by some design. If I had rung a bell and announced to the empty air, "I am ready once again to initiate beginners into the art of meditation and imagery," I couldn't have had a better response. As that kind of activity was furthest from my thoughts and desires at that time, I was taken by surprise when virtual strangers, one after the other, approached me with such a request — strangers who knew very little about me and certainly had no idea of what had been happening to me lately. Some I met casually, some only knew me as the author of *The Bright Light of Death*. They did not know they were requesting something of me which I had terminated some years ago — they didn't even know my age. A few years ago, when I conducted my last group meeting, I was convinced that my active days were over. I knew that younger leaders were available and ready to serve. I thought I was too old. Philosophically and cheerfully I accepted the edict of nature.

But my special protection during the California earthquake, following so quickly after the last experience of vibratory healings, made me realize that I was wrong. All the old opinions of myself didn't matter, time didn't matter, age didn't matter — nothing of that kind mattered. That was not important! There was still something for me to do. The next step would be shown to me commensurate with my abilities.

The first inkling I got of a direction came in a following meditation. I had no sooner relaxed, asking for "what is right and best" at this time, than an image appeared of a railroad crossing with the signs reading. "Stop/Look/Listen." Once before, many years ago, I had received the same symbols, again in answer to a similar question asking for directions. Instead of terminating my activities, I seemed to be told to stop and wait for the signal (I recognized the symbology used by the Inner Teacher showing me my next step). I stopped and watched as the train went by with passengers peering out of the windows, waving to me, and then stopping nearby. I continued watching as some of them got off and approached me. They seemed as though they were old friends. We belonged together. This small group became the nucleus of my next class.

As time went on, the image of the railroad crossing became more significant. The small group who had disembarked was just a beginning, as more and more people kept coming. Not only new people, but also former students and associates, appeared as though by some orderly and well-orchestrated design. Besides wishing to learn how to meditate and visualize, they were anxious to solve major problems in their lives. Coincidentally, most of their problems involved relationships. The process explained in chapters V and VI, "Healing the Past," was directly applicable in many cases. And at this moment in time, I could honestly subscribe to this unique process as a proven success.

A major problem for me now became one of logistics — I couldn't handle it alone. A few days later, a solution flashed through my mind — "The right people at the right time!" Two of my best friends came readily to mind as the ideal answer for the solution to my dilemma. Both of them were trained psychologists, and they knew firsthand the process described in "Healing the Past."

I had met J. L. less than a year ago, and from the first

moment, we both recognized a meeting of the mind and heart. On a deep inner level there was a coherency of thought, a depth of understanding and an unusual bond of connectedness. By training and background, she is the ideal counselor, with a lifetime of experience in heart-ache and rejection by both parents. When I asked her if she would be interested in learning how to include the healing-of-the-past process in her curriculum, she enthusiastically assented. By training and personal experience, she profoundly understands mother-child problems.

I am blessed with another friend, a highly qualified psychologist. I have intimately known Dr. L. for a great many years. We worked together many times, particularly in situations involving mother-daughter-son relationships. In retrospect, this was significant. She excels in imagery, is innovative, highly intuitive and has a brilliant mind. When I asked her if she would like to join me in further studying the latest procedures, she, too, enthusiastically endorsed the idea. We agreed to set time aside for further study.

The fact that these two friends — qualified therapists — were cooperative was encouraging, and the fact that the new classes were organized so easily and speedily was another sign to me that I should continue as long as possible. The students seeking knowledge of advanced meditation and a better way to handle their problems learned that it was of utmost importance to focus on making a connection with the High Self, the Soul. From the beginning I emphasized that *that* connection was the chief aim of advanced meditation and they were to devote their daily meditations to the achievement of that goal. I know of no better way to become more aware, more intuitive, wiser and more loving.

And I was at peace knowing that I was following the guidance of the Inner Teacher, doing what I was supposed to do. It all seemed right.

Epilogue

Although this book is an account of my experiences in healing, both physical and emotional, the main purpose of writing — and for me, the only important purpose — has been to present evidence of the Presence of the Light, the forces of Good. We have come to a time in human history when experiences of this kind should be told. Such experiences are happening to people like me — far from pure, far from perfect, and yet a channel for receiving evidence of the power of the Light.

The message is clearer to me than my ability to transmit it. My convictions have always come from the teachings of the Inner Teacher, which are unfailingly wise, true, honest. I have no doubts. In these latter years of my life, I am willing to transmit the teaching without false modesty and excuses.

Questions and Answers

Q.   The Light—some people claim to see it as they are dying. Is that true?

A.   Definitely, yes. It is called by many names—the Light of the Soul, the Guardian Angel; it is there at death to help the dead over the threshold. Many people claim to have seen it. The dying are often surprised that other people in the room don't also see it, but it is usually visible only to the dying one.

Q.   Did you eve see the Light again as you described in your first chapter?

A.   No, not in the same way. There were other unusual mystical experiences, such as the advent of the Universal Mother (see ch. VI).

Q.   Why not?

A.   I honestly doubt if my mind and body could take that powerful energy often. Maybe I am not advanced enough, or maybe the planet earth is not suitable for so much voltage of power. I don't know.

Q. Could I or anyone telephone you and ask for a phone treatment?

A. No. I cannot choose or command or make the vibrations that instigated the healings in chapter VIII. The vibrations have a life of their own. They are in and around us all the time. I believe that some day all of us will learn how to vibrate in harmony with the positive and good energy for better health and happier living. We have many lessons to learn first.

Q. Do you know people who are teaching how to bring good vibrations, or energy, into our lives?

A. Yes. Many. There are many books on this subject and many groups studying energy fields.

Q. How can I start?

A. From the beginning. Start with meditation. The goal of meditation is to connect with the energy of the Universe, the energy of love and wisdom.

Q. I have a friend who began to hallucinate after prolonged meditations. Is that possible?

A. Yes. You said *prolonged* meditations (such as six or eight hours daily). This is unnatural in many ways, and certainly not beneficial. We have to function in *this* world — provide for our daily sustenance, attend to obligations; this is why we are here. Going off the deep end in order to get to Heaven quickly can get you going in the opposite direction — quickly.

Q. Many times in your book you mention the danger of coercion, of giving your will over to the power of another, etc. Isn't that what followers do all the time?

A. That is an important thing to watch for in any leader—particularly a spiritual leader. A wise leader, or teacher, suggests, points out the various ways to go, but *never* tells you what to do, never twists your mind to obey him, never bends you to his will. If you should ever fall into that trap, run away as fast as you can. You are not a slave!

Q. I would like to experience the mystical union. Is there any way you can help me?

A. The mystical union cannot be transferred. Professor William James of Harvard, an authority on the subject of mystical states, investigated many mystics and their experiences. He wrote: "The mystical state must be directly experienced . . . [it is] seemingly beyond concrete knowledge resulting in a depth of insight carrying within a curious sense of authority for aftertime. It cannot be transferred." (See *The Varieties of Religious Experience*).

Q. You write that you began meditating forty years ago. I found that after a few years, I dropped it. Don't you ever get bored with it?

A. No. Never. After a few years, as time went on, it became an important part of my daily routine; it gives me a feeling of well-being and energy. Daily meditation is a creative process that manifests in many ways. I can't do without it.

Q. Did you do other healings besides those in the book?
A. Yes. Many.

Q. Were there failures?
A. Yes, of course.

Q. Were you ever embarrassed or discouraged by the failures?
A. Fortunately, not. I always knew that I was just a conduit for the higher energy, the God force. Because of this understanding, I never felt personally responsible for the successes or the failures.

Q. Do I have to reach a state of perfection or piety to experience a oneness with the Light?
A. No, not at all. If perfection were the requirement, I would not have been a candidate.

Q. Many times you refer to the vibrations or power of the Light. Can you enlarge on that?
A. Yes. The power of the Light is *always* here in our environment, often physically experienced as a vibration. In its positive influence, it becomes a love-wisdom connection; in its negative influence, it is undesirable and, in the final analysis, destructive. Since we attract what is in our nature, it is vitally important for all of us to free the little self (the

ego) of all desire for self-aggrandizement, self-importance, selfish gains. The purity of our purpose determines the extent of individual growth and rise as a partner of the Universal Goodness. There is an enormous need today for more such candidates to offset the preponderance of anger, greed and violence in the world. The choice is ours.

Suggested Reading

A Brief History of Time, by Stephen Hawking

Breakthrough to Creativity, by Shafica Karagulla

Chakras and the Human Energy Fields, by Shafica Karagulla & Dora Kunz

Cosmic Consciousness, by Richard M. Bucke

Einstein's Dreams, by Alan Lightman

Human Personality and Its Survival of Bodily Death, by F. W. H. Myers

Life After Life, by Dr. Raymond Moody

Man, Visible and Invisible, by C. W. Leadbeater

Many Lives, Many Masters, by Brian Weiss

Memories, Dreams, Reflections, by C. G. Jung

Mystical Qabalah, by Dion Fortune

Psychic Self-Defense, by Dion Fortune

Quantum Healing, by Deepak Chopra

Search in Secret India, by Paul Brunton

The Celestine Prophecy, by James Redfield

The Dancing WuLi Masters, by Gary Zukav

The Presence of the Past, by Rupert Sheldrake

The Seat of the Soul, by Gary Zukav

The Unobstructed Universe, by Stewart E. White

The Varieties of Religious Experience, by William James

There Is a River—The Story of Edgar Cayce, by Thomas Sugrue